THE LIFE OF SOJOURNER TRUTH

BY GILLIA M. OLSON

SEQUENCE

AMICUS | AMICUS INK

Sequence is published by Amicus and Amicus Ink
P.O. Box 227, Mankato, MN 56002
www.amicuspublishing.us

Library of Congress Cataloging-in-Publication Data
Names: Olson, Gillia M., author.
Title: The life of Sojourner Truth / by Gillia M. Olson.
Description: Mankato, MN : Amicus, [2022] | Series: Change maker biographies | Includes bibliographical references and index. | Audience: Grades 2–3 | Audience: Ages 7–10
Identifiers: LCCN 2019036339 (print) | LCCN 2019036340 (ebook) | ISBN 9781681519524 (library binding) | ISBN 9781681525990 (paperback) | ISBN 9781645490371 (pdf)
Subjects: LCSH: Truth, Sojourner, 1799–1883–Juvenile literature. | African American abolitionists–Biography–Juvenile literature. | Abolitionists–United States–Biography–Juvenile literature. | African American women–Biography–Juvenile literature. | Social reformers–United States–Biography–Juvenile literature.
Classification: LCC E185.97.T8 O47 2022 (print) | LCC E185.97.T8 (ebook) | DDC 326/.8092 [B]–dc23
LC record available at https://lccn.loc.gov/2019036339
LC ebook record available at https://lccn.loc.gov/2019036340

Editor: Alissa Thielges
Designer: Ciara Beitlich
Photo Researcher: Marty Levick and Bridget Prehn

Photo Credits: Shutterstock/Everett Historical cover; Wikimedia/Mathew Brady cover; Getty/Bettmann 4, 8; Getty/Hulton Archive/Stringer 6–7; Getty/Photos.com 11; Flickr/Wally Gobetz 12; Wikimedia/Ulster County Clerk 12–13; LOC/ Dubourg, M., engraver 14–15; Getty/Universal History Archive 17, 18; LOC/Sojourner Truth, Eastern District, Michigan 18; Wikimedia/Randall Studio 21; Getty/MPI/Stringer 21; LOC 22–23; Getty/Universal Images Group 25; LOC/Carroll's Art Gallery 26; Getty/Chip Somodevilla 28–29

TABLE OF CONTENTS

Though she could not read or write, Sojourner Truth was a powerful speaker.

LOADING . . . LOADING . . . LOADING . . .

Who was Sojourner Truth?

Sojourner Truth faced big barriers. She was an African American born into **slavery**. Women in her time had few rights. But Sojourner Truth had **faith**. Her faith moved her to change the world. She became a **preacher**. She worked for rights for African Americans and women. She is one of the best-known speakers of the 19th century.

LOADING . . . LOADING . . . LOADING . . .

Sojourner was born in New York in about 1797. Her original name was Isabella. Her parents were enslaved. Like most slaves, Isabella did not learn to read or write. Her mother was a **Christian**. She taught her children to pray.

Isabella was sold several times as a child. In 1810, she was sold to the Dumonts. They would be her last "owners."

A woman is sold at a slave auction. African Americans were often sold in this manner.

Sojourner is born into slavery in New York.

1797

LOADING... LOADING...

LOADING... LOADING... LOADING...

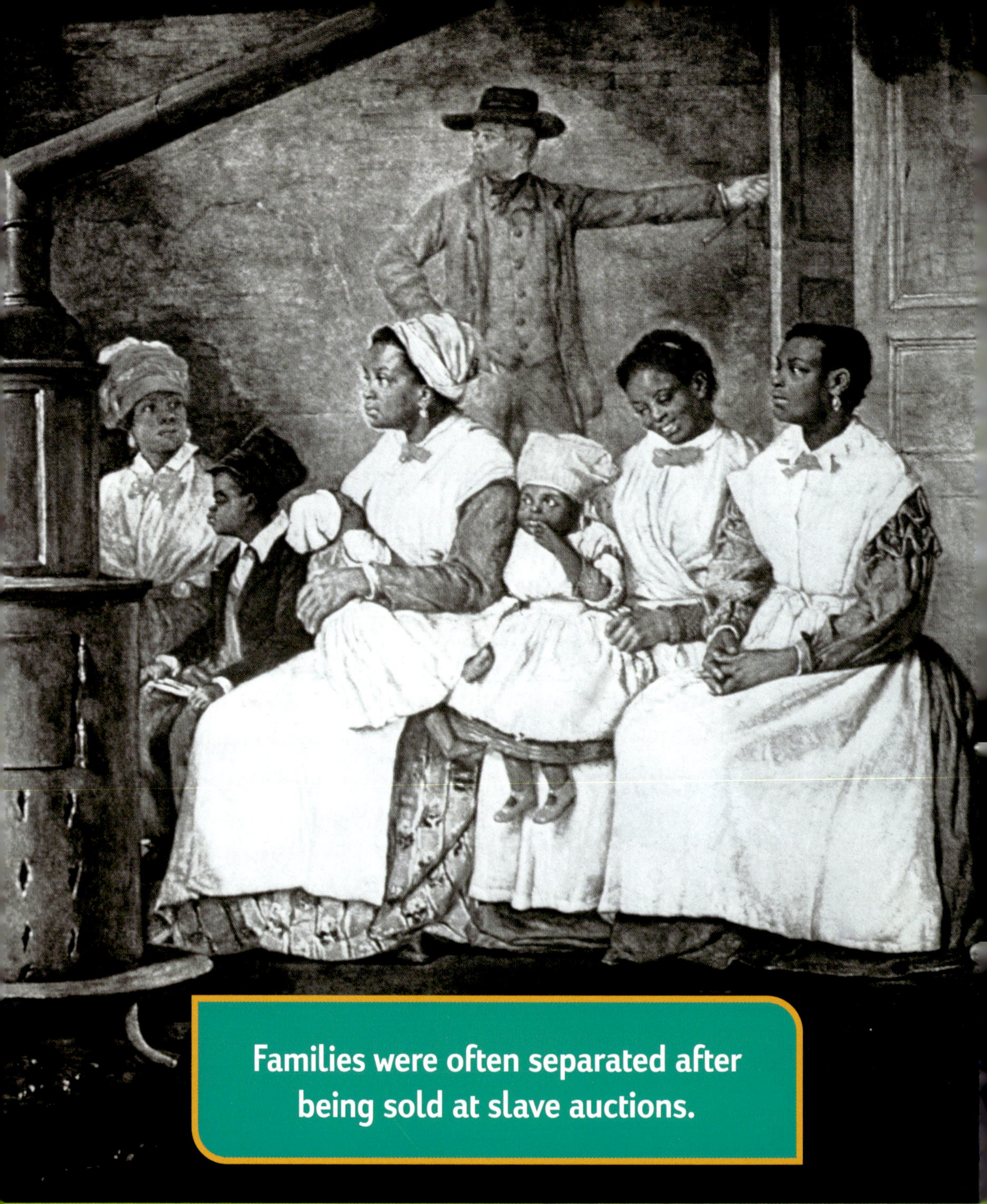

Families were often separated after being sold at slave auctions.

Sojourner is born into slavery in New York.

1797

1815

Isabella marries Thomas.

LOADING... LOADING...

In 1815, Isabella married Thomas. He was also enslaved by the Dumonts. By 1826, Isabella had five children. The next year, slavery ended in New York for adults. Children were still enslaved until at least age 25. The Dumonts had promised to free Isabella in 1826. She and Thomas were going live on Dumont land with their children. But the Dumonts did not free them.

LOADING . . . LOADING . . . LOADING . . .

Leaving Slavery

Isabella felt that God told her to leave the Dumonts. In late 1826, Isabella packed up her youngest, Sophia. They left on foot. The other children stayed with Thomas at the Dumonts. Isabella met Isaac and Maria Van Wagenen. They gave her **refuge**. Soon, John Dumont came looking for Isabella. The Van Wagenens bought Isabella's and Sophia's freedom.

1797 — Sojourner is born into slavery in New York.

1815 — Isabella marries Thomas.

1826 — Isabella leaves the Dumont farm, escaping from slavery.

. . . LOADING . . .

A woman escapes slavery with her baby, like Isabella did with Sophia.

LOADING . . . LOADING . . . LOADING . . .

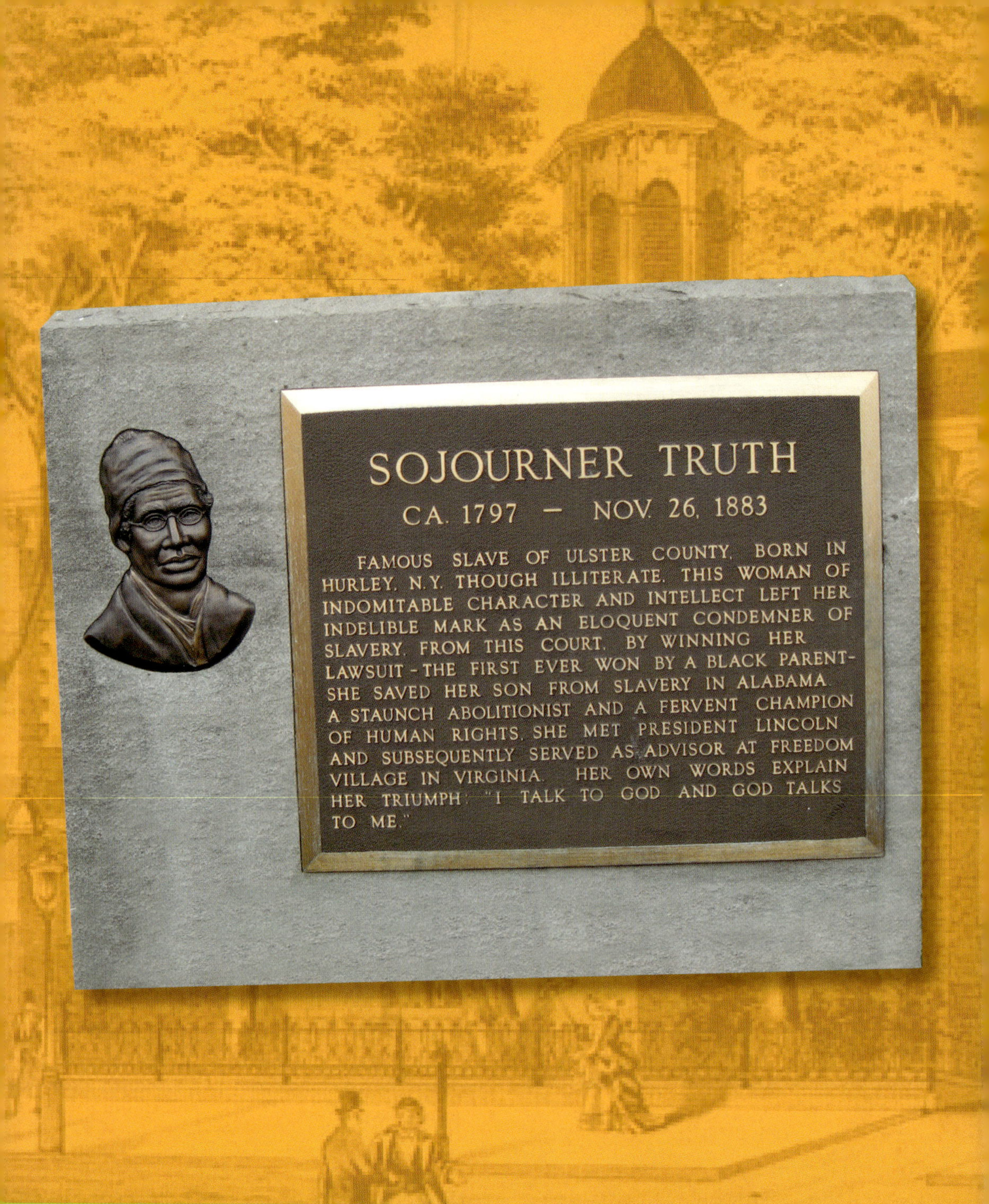

1797 – Sojourner is born into slavery in New York.

1815 – Isabella marries Thomas.

1826 – Isabella leaves the Dumont farm, escaping from slavery.

1828 – Isbella successfully sues to get her son back from slavery in Alabama.

After Isabella left, her son Peter was sold. He was only five. He ended up in Alabama. This sale was illegal. New York slaves could not be sold to states that would have slavery after 1827. Isabella was horrified. She **sued** to get Peter back. She won! He was freed from slavery in 1828. The case was famous. For the first time, a black woman sued a white man and won.

A plaque is outside the courthouse where Sojourner won her son back.

In 1828, Isabella moved to New York City. Peter and Sophia went with her. By law, her other daughters had to stay at the Dumonts. Isabella worked as a housekeeper. She went to church. She also went to Christian camp meetings. Isabella preached. She was known for her powerful speaking and singing voice.

Sojourner preached at camp meetings like this one in the 1820s.

- 1797 — Sojourner is born into slavery in New York.
- 1815 — Isabella marries Thomas.
- 1826 — Isabella leaves the Dumont farm, escaping from slavery.
- 1828 — Isbella successfully sues to get her son back from slavery in Alabama.
- 1828 — Isabella moves to New York.

LOADING... LOADING... LOADING...

Becoming Sojourner Truth

Isabella lived in New York for 15 years. Her faith stayed strong. In 1843, she felt the Holy Spirit call to her. She changed her name to Sojourner Truth. A sojourner is a visitor. It was a fitting name. She traveled around. She visited towns and preached. Crowds loved her. Many people became Christians after hearing her speak.

- **1797** Sojourner is born into slavery in New York.
- **1815** Isabella marries Thomas.
- **1826** Isabella leaves the Dumont farm, escaping from slavery.
- **1828** Isbella successfully sues to get her son back from slavery in Alabama.
- **1828** Isabella moves to New York.
- **1843** Isabella changes name to Sojourner Truth; travels as a preacher.

Sojourner reaches out to the crowd during a speech.

LOADING... LOADING... LOADING...

- **1797** Sojourner is born into slavery in New York.
- **1815** Isabella marries Thomas.
- **1826** Isabella leaves the Dumont farm, escaping from slavery.
- **1828** Isbella successfully sues to get her son back from slavery in Alabama.
- **1828** Isabella moves to New York.
- **1843** Isabella changes name to Sojourner Truth; travels as a preacher.

In 1844, Sojourner moved to Northampton, Massachusetts. About 300 people lived there. They were all were equal. Men and women of all races worked together. Speakers talked about ending slavery and women's rights. Sojourner was inspired. She was already a great speaker. Now, she began to speak about equal rights.

Sojourner sold photos of herself to help pay for her travels.

Sojourner moves to Northampton, Massachusetts.

1844

. . L O A D I N G . . . L O A D I N G . . .

Slavery and Women's Rights

In 1846, Sojourner started a book about her life. She told her story to Olive Gilbert, who wrote it down. The book was published in 1850. In 1851, she spoke at the Women's Rights Convention in Ohio. Her speech was later called, "Ain't I a Woman?" She said she worked as hard as a man. Black women deserved as many rights as white men.

- 1797: Sojourner is born into slavery in New York.
- 1815: Isabella marries Thomas.
- 1826: Isabella leaves the Dumont farm, escaping from slavery.
- 1828: Isbella successfully sues to get her son back from slavery in Alabama.
- 1828: Isabella moves to New York.
- 1843: Isabella changes name to Sojourner Truth; travels as a preacher.

NARRATIVE

OF

SOJOURNER TRUTH,

A

NORTHERN SLAVE,

EMANCIPATED FROM BODILY SERVITUDE BY THE STATE OF NEW YORK, IN 1828.

WITH A PORTRAIT.

'Sweet is the virgin honey, though the wild bee store it in a reed;
And bright the jewelled band that circleth an Ethiop's arm;
Pure are the grains of gold in the turbid stream of the Ganges;
And fair the living flowers that spring from the dull cold sod.
Wherefore, thou gentle student, bend thine ear to my speech,
For I also am as thou art; our hearts can commune together:
To meanest matters will I stoop, for mean is the lot of mortal;
I will rise to noblest themes, for the soul hath a heritage of glory.'

BOSTON:
PRINTED FOR THE AUTHOR.
1850.

Sojourner's book is called *Narrative of Sojourner Truth.* She sold it at places she spoke.

Sojourner moves to Northampton, Massachusetts.

1844

1851

...DING . . . LOADING . . .

Sojourner gives "Ain't I a Woman?" speech.

1797	1815	1826	1828	1828	1843
Sojourner is born into slavery in New York.	Isabella marries Thomas.	Isabella leaves the Dumont farm, escaping from slavery.	Isbella successfully sues to get her son back from slavery in Alabama.	Isabella moves to New York.	Isabella changes name to Sojourner Truth; travels as a preacher.

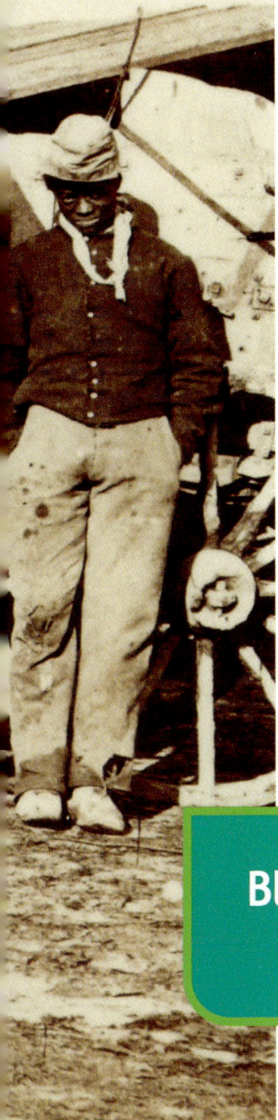

Sojourner continued to speak around the country. She drew large crowds. In 1857, friends convinced her to move to Michigan. Her daughters, now free, moved there, too.

The **U.S. Civil War** began in 1861. Sojourner **recruited** black troops. She gathered food and clothing. She sent these to black soldiers.

Black soldiers fought for the Union in the Civil War to end slavery.

1844 — Sojourner moves to Northampton, Massachusetts.

1851 — Sojourner gives "Ain't I a Woman?" speech.

1857 — Sojourner moves to Michigan.

...LOADING...

Helping the Newly Free

Sojourner went to Washington, D.C., in 1864. She wanted to help the war effort in the capital. She met President Abraham Lincoln.

Sojourner stayed in Washington for a while. She **counseled** newly-freed slaves. They needed jobs and training. She helped some move to new places.

Lincoln shows Sojourner a Bible he received from African Americans.

1797	Sojourner is born into slavery in New York.
1815	Isabella marries Thomas.
1826	Isabella leaves the Dumont farm, escaping from slavery.
1828	Isbella successfully sues to get her son back from slavery in Alabama.
1828	Isabella moves to New York.
1843	Isabella changes name to Sojourner Truth; travels as a preacher.

Sojourner moves to Northampton, Massachusetts.

Sojourner moves to Michigan.

1844

1851

1857

1864

LOADING . . .

Sojourner gives "Ain't I a Woman?" speech.

Sojourner goes to Washington, D.C., and meets Lincoln.

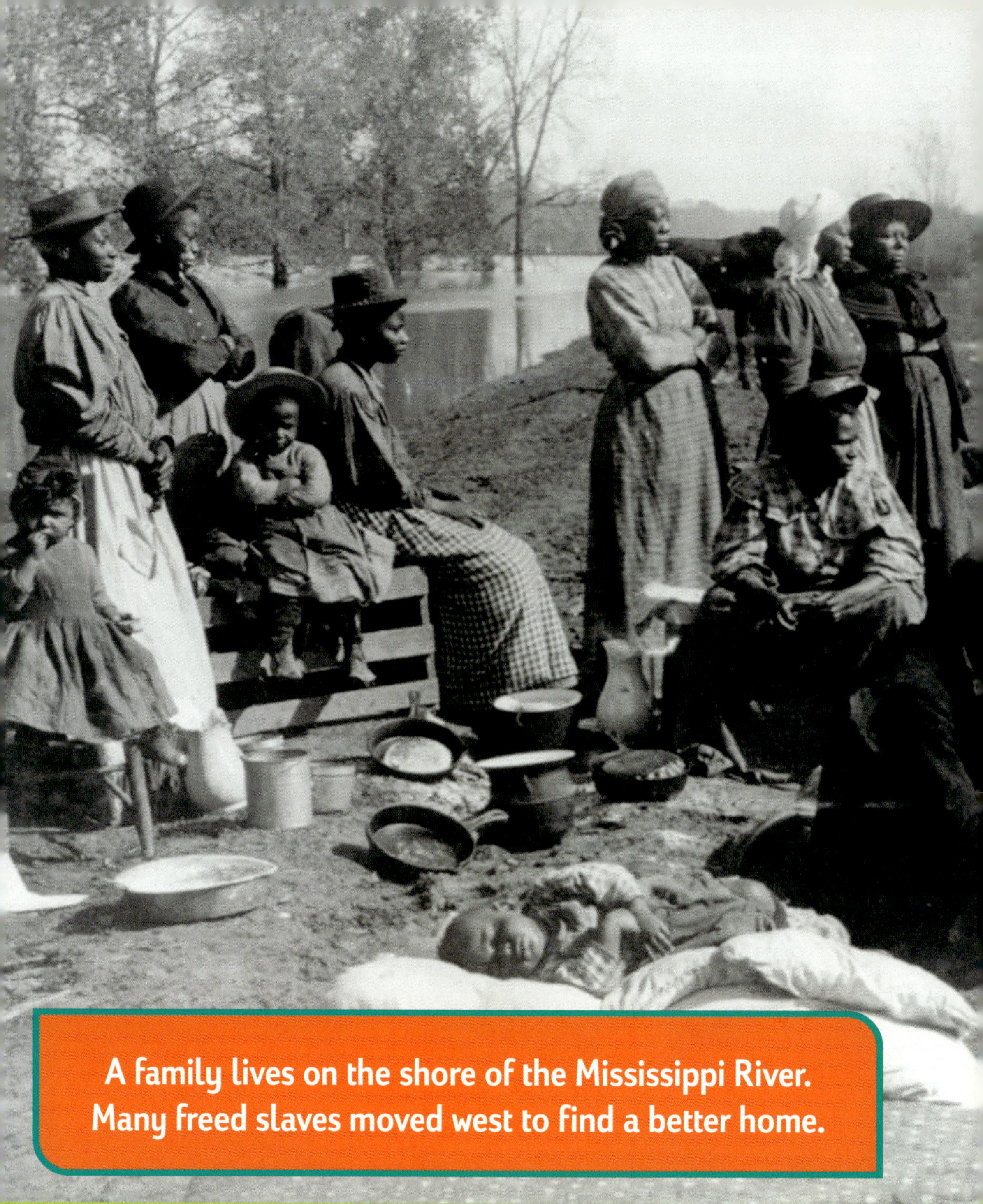

A family lives on the shore of the Mississippi River. Many freed slaves moved west to find a better home.

- 1797 — Sojourner is born into slavery in New York.
- 1815 — Isabella marries Thomas.
- 1826 — Isabella leaves the Dumont farm, escaping from slavery.
- 1828 — Isbella successfully sues to get her son back from slavery in Alabama.
- 1828 — Isabella moves to New York.
- 1843 — Isabella changes name to Sojourner Truth; travels as a preacher.

Sojourner continued to preach. She spoke for voting rights and help for African Americans. She wanted freed slaves to have a place of their own. Land in the west was still open. That would work perfectly, she thought. In 1879, groups of freed people went to Kansas. Sojourner helped them. She felt God had answered her prayers.

- 1844 — Sojourner moves to Northampton, Massachusetts.
- 1851 — Sojourner gives "Ain't I a Woman?" speech.
- 1857 — Sojourner moves to Michigan.
- 1864 — Sojourner goes to Washington, D.C., and meets Lincoln.
- 1879 — Sojourner helps former slaves move to Kansas.

NG . . .

Sojourner died at home in Battle Creek, Michigan, in 1883. She was 86. Many people went to her funeral. In 2009, a **bust** of her was placed in the U.S. Capitol. She was the first African American woman to have that honor. Sojourner is remembered for her ability to speak to all people. Her faith helped her fight for equal rights.

Sojourner Truth's bronze bust is unveiled in the Capitol in Washington, D.C.

1797 — Sojourner is born into slavery in New York.

1815 — Isabella marries Thomas.

1826 — Isabella leaves the Dumont farm, escaping from slavery.

1828 — Isbella successfully sues to get her son back from slavery in Alabama.

1828 — Isabella moves to New York.

1843 — Isabella changes name to Sojourner Truth; travels as a preacher.

1844	1851	1857	1864	1879	1883
Sojourner moves to Northampton, Massachusetts.	Sojourner gives "Ain't I a Woman?" speech.	Sojourner moves to Michigan.	Sojourner goes to Washington, D.C., and meets Lincoln.	Sojourner helps former slaves move to Kansas.	Sojourner dies in Battle Creek, Michigan.

Glossary

bust A sculpture of a person's head and shoulders.

Christian Someone who believes Jesus is the son of God and follows his teachings.

counsel To listen to someone's problems and give advice.

faith Belief and trust in God.

preacher A person who speaks publicly about religion.

recruit To get someone to join a group or cause.

refuge Protection or shelter from danger or trouble.

slavery When people are owned by another person and can be sold at the owner's will.

sue To seek justice from someone by taking legal action against them.

U.S. Civil War A war from 1861 to 1865 between the northern and southern states of the United States over the enslavement of African Americans.

Read More

Schmidt, Gary D. *So Tall Within: Sojourner Truth's Long Walk Toward Freedom.* New York: Roaring Brook Press, 2018.

Susienka, Kristen. *Sojourner Truth.* New York: PowerKids Press, 2020.

Taylor, Charlotte. *Sojourner Truth: Abolitionist and Activist.* Exceptional African Americans. New York: Enslow Publishing, 2016.

Websites

National Women's History Museum | Sojourner Truth
https://www.womenshistory.org/exhibits/sojourner-truth

PBS Learning Media: Sojourner Truth
https://www.pbslearningmedia.org/resource/americon-vid-sojourner-truth/sojourner-truth/

The Sojourner Truth Project: The Readings
https://www.thesojournertruthproject.com/the-readings/

Every effort has been made to ensure that these websites are appropriate for children. However, because of the nature of the Internet, it is impossible to guarantee that these sites will remain active indefinitely or that their contents will not be altered.

Index

About the Author

Gillia M. Olson is a former farm girl turned writer. She's written and edited children's books for more than 20 years. She hopes stories of great women will inspire her daughter someday, just as they have inspired her. She lives in southern Minnesota.